from SEA TO SHINING SEA

WEST VIRGINIA

By Dennis Brindell Fradin and Judith Bloom Fradin

CONSULTANTS

Christine M. Kreiser, M.A., Historian, West Virginia State Archives;
Assistant Editor, *West Virginia History*

Robert L. Hillerich, Ph.D., Professor Emeritus, Bowling Green State University;
Consultant, Pinellas County Schools, Florida

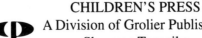

CHILDREN'S PRESS
A Division of Grolier Publishing
Sherman Turnpike
Danbury, Connecticut 06816

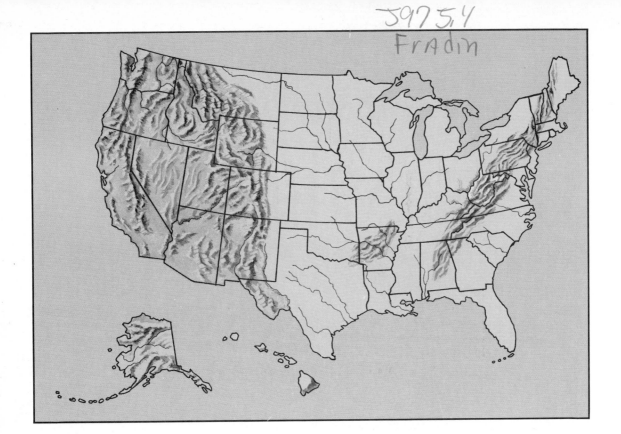

West Virginia is one of the fourteen states in the region called the South. The other southern states are Alabama, Arkansas, Delaware, Florida, Georgia, Kentucky, Louisiana, Maryland, Mississippi, North Carolina, South Carolina, Tennessee, and Virginia.

For our dear friend, Carol Green Bloom

Front cover picture: The Governor's Mansion, Charleston; page 1: New River Gorge, New River Gorge National River; back cover: Glade Creek Grist Mill, Babcock State Park

Project Editor: Joan Downing
Design Director: Karen Kohn
Typesetting: Graphic Connections, Inc.
Engraving: Liberty Photoengraving

Library of Congress Cataloging-in-Publication Data

Fradin, Dennis B.
  West Virginia / by Dennis Brindell Fradin & Judith
Bloom Fradin.
    p.   cm. — (From sea to shining sea)
  Includes index.
  ISBN 0-516-03848-6
    1. West Virginia—Juvenile literature. [1. West Virginia.]
I. Fradin, Judith Bloom. II. Title. III. Series: Fradin,
Dennis B. From sea to shining sea.
F241.3.F72   1994   94-17016
975—dc20   CIP
                                                          AC

Table of Contents

Children playing soccer in Kanawha County

Introducing the Mountain State

West Virginia lies in the southern part of the United States. The state is covered with hills and highlands. Its nickname is the "Mountain State." The state motto is "Mountaineers Are Always Free." That shows West Virginians' love of freedom.

West Virginia started out as the western part of Virginia. From 1776, western Virginians had wanted to have their own state. When Virginia left the Union in 1861, western Virginians refused to follow. West Virginia entered the Union as a separate state in 1863.

Today, West Virginians are known as great coal producers. The state's workers also make chemicals, metals, and glassware. West Virginia farmers are known for their apples and peaches.

The Mountain State is special in other ways, too. Where were General "Stonewall" Jackson and gymnast Mary Lou Retton born? Where did the great black leader Booker T. Washington grow up? Where did John Henry's contest against a machine take place? The answer to these questions is: West Virginia!

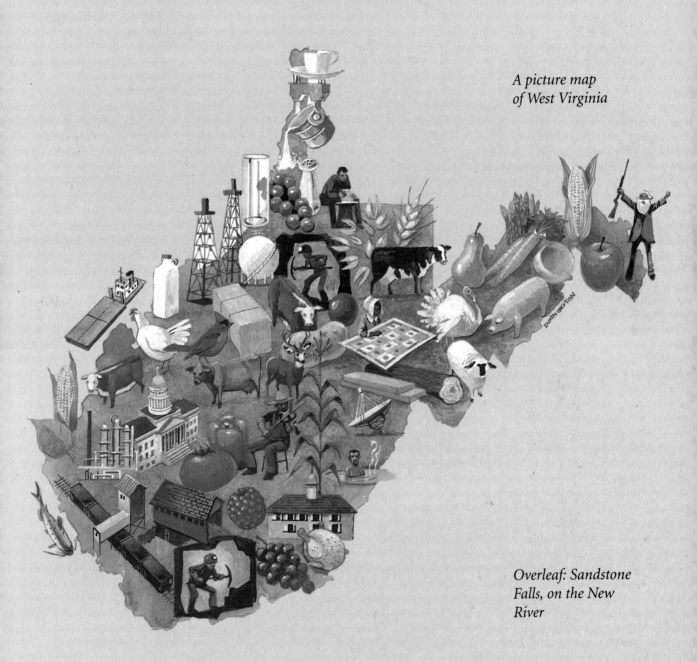

*A picture map
of West Virginia*

*Overleaf: Sandstone
Falls, on the New
River*

5

"*Oh, the West Virginia Hills!*"

"Oh, the West Virginia Hills!"

West Virginia covers 24,231 square miles. Forty states are larger. Only nine are smaller. West Virginia is one of the oddest-shaped states. It almost looks like an apron. The Northern Panhandle and Eastern Panhandle are the apron's ties.

The Northern Panhandle makes West Virginia the northernmost of the southern states. Ohio lies to the northwest. Pennsylvania and Maryland are to the north and east. Virginia is south and southeast of the Mountain State. Kentucky is to the southwest.

"Oh, the West Virginia hills! How majestic and how grand . . ." These words begin one of West Virginia's state songs. West Virginia is the only state completely within the Appalachian Mountains. Its many mountains and hills make the state's average height 1,500 feet. Spruce Knob, at 4,863 feet, is West Virginia's highest point.

Water, Woods, and Wildlife

Rivers wind along much of the state's borders. The Ohio River twists for nearly 300 miles along the

The Northern Panhandle's tip is only about 100 miles from Canada.

Seneca Rocks, in Spruce Knob-Seneca Rocks National Recreation Area

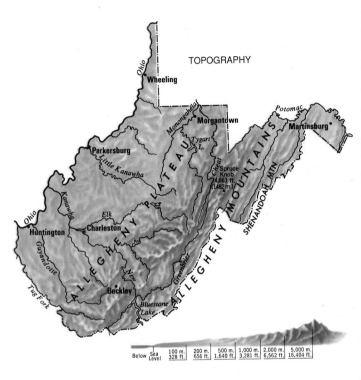

TOPOGRAPHY

Wheeling

Morgantown

Tygart L.

Parkersburg

Little Kanawha

Spruce Knob 4,863 ft. (1,482 m.)

Martinsburg

Potomac

ALLEGHENY PLATEAU

ALLEGHENY MOUNTAINS

SHENANDOAH MTN.

Ohio

Kanawha

Elk

Charleston

Huntington

Guyandotte

New

Greenbrier

Beckley

Tug Fork

Bluestone Lake

Below Sea Level | 100 m. 328 ft. | 200 m. 656 ft. | 500 m. 1,640 ft. | 1,000 m. 3,281 ft. | 2,000 m. 6,562 ft. | 5,000 m. 16,404 ft.

border with Ohio. The Potomac River forms most of the border with Maryland. The Big Sandy and Tug Fork rivers separate Kentucky from West Virginia. Major rivers also flow within the state. They include the Kanawha, Little Kanawha, New, and Greenbrier. Other rivers were dammed to create big lakes. The Elk River was dammed to form Sutton Lake. Summersville Lake was formed on the Gauley River. West Virginia has no big natural lakes.

About 80 percent of West Virginia is wooded. The sugar maple is the state tree. Pines, spruces,

Left: A view of the New River Gorge

Bloodroot

Fall colors reflected in a Pendleton County farm pond

oaks, and poplars also grow in the Mountain State. Many wildflowers grow in West Virginia's meadows and woods. The rhododendron is the state flower. Other wildflowers are the bloodroot and dogwood. West Virginia is home to many animals. The black bear is the state animal. Deer, foxes, opossums, and skunks are among the state's other animals. The cardinal is the state bird. Eagles, owls, hawks, crows, and catbirds are among its other birds. The brook trout is the state fish. It is found in mountain streams.

CLIMATE

Winter on Spruce Knob

A rather mild climate favors West Virginia. Summers are not as hot as in states farther south. Winters are not as cold as in places farther north. Temperatures are around 80 degrees Fahrenheit in summer. Winter temperatures close to 30 degrees Fahrenheit are common. But it is always cooler in the mountains.

Barn owl

Plentiful rain helps the state's crops grow. But summer storms sometimes cause flash floods. Fog often blankets the river valleys. Snowfall is less than 2 feet a year in the southwest. Almost 10 feet of snow can fall in the mountains.

From Ancient Times Until Today

FROM ANCIENT TIMES UNTIL TODAY

Over 300 million years ago, swamps covered West Virginia. Plants lived in the water. As they died, layers of plants formed peat. This hardened into coal.

West Virginia's mountains and valleys were formed about 70 million years ago. The Appalachians are America's oldest mountains. They were folded and pushed up out of the earth.

Opposite: These Civilian Conservation Corps (CCC) workers lived at Camp Marshall, near Moundsville, during the Great Depression.

NATIVE AMERICANS

People first reached West Virginia around 16,000 years ago. These ancient Indians hunted with spears. In time, they learned to farm. About 2,500 years ago, some Indians began building huge dirt mounds. They were used as burial places and as platforms for buildings. Grave Creek Mound is in the Northern Panhandle. It is seven stories high. Its base is 900 feet around.

By the 1600s, several groups of Indians lived in West Virginia. They included the Cherokee, Conoy, Susquehanna, Shawnee, Delaware, and Iroquois. Some Indians built villages along West Virginia's

Grave Creek Mound

Virginians Thomas Batts and Robert Fallam explored along the New River in 1671.

rivers. Others came there just to hunt or gather salt. The land was too mountainous for much farming.

EXPLORERS AND SETTLERS

In 1607, England founded the first of its thirteen American colonies. The colony was called Virginia. Present-day West Virginia was then part of Virginia. It was known as western Virginia.

John Lederer is thought to have been the first explorer to enter western Virginia. He arrived near present-day Harpers Ferry in 1669. Thomas Batts and Robert Fallam arrived in 1671. These two Virginians explored along the New River.

Nearly sixty years passed before people settled in western Virginia. In 1727, German people headed south from Pennsylvania. They settled in western Virginia's Eastern Panhandle. They named their new settlement Mecklenburg after a town in Germany. Today, Mecklenburg is called Shepherdstown. Around 1731, Morgan ap Morgan came to western Virginia. He was a Welshman from Delaware. Morgan built a log cabin at Bunker Hill. More settlers arrived from other colonies. Settlers also came from England, Ireland, Scotland, and Germany.

The cabin of Morgan ap Morgan, one of western Virginia's earliest permanent settlers

Mountains separated western Virginia from Virginia and the rest of the colonies. Settlers in the west had to fend for themselves. Families chopped down trees. They used the wood to build log cabins and furniture. For food, they planted corn, hunted deer, and fished. They made their own clothing, soap, and candles. The pioneers made corn-husk brooms to clean their cabins. They carved apple-head dolls for their children.

During these early years, the settlers took over Indian lands. Fights broke out between the two groups. Forts were built in western Virginia to protect the settlers. Some grew into cities. In 1767, Zackquill Morgan and other settlers built Fort Kern

Zackquill Morgan was Morgan ap Morgan's son.

15

and Fort Morgan. Their settlement grew into Morgantown. Fort Henry was begun in 1774. It helped Wheeling become a major town. Fort Lee was built in 1788. It marked the start of Charleston.

GUNFIRE IN THE HILLS

Lord Dunmore

Logan was a Mingo leader in the Northern Panhandle. He had always lived peacefully among the settlers. On April 30, 1774, drunken settlers murdered his family. Logan went on the warpath. So did Cornstalk, a Shawnee chief. Virginia governor Lord Dunmore sent troops into western Virginia. That is how Lord Dunmore's War started.

On October 10, 1774, the war ended. The settlers defeated Chief Cornstalk's forces. The battle took place at what is now Point Pleasant. Treaties were signed. The settlers had gained control of western Virginia.

About 30,000 settlers lived in western Virginia by 1776. Also in 1776, the thirteen colonies broke from England. By that time, western Virginians wanted to separate from Virginia. But they didn't. Instead, they helped the United States win the Revolutionary War (1775-1783). About 1,300 western Virginians fought for independence.

Many Indians in western Virginia helped England. They led attacks on settlers throughout the war. Some Indians had scalped a settler near Point Pleasant. Other settlers wanted revenge. Chief Cornstalk and his son then arrived at Point Pleasant in 1777. They came to talk peace. But some settlers killed Cornstalk, his son, and several other Shawnees.

The Americans won the Revolutionary War. The United States then owned all land east of the Mississippi. People in western Virginia had helped protect that land.

A Revolutionary War reenactment at Blennerhassett Island State Park

Natural Resources and Transportation

By 1790, western Virginia had about 56,000 people. They began to make use of the land's treasures. Peter Tarr built an ironworks in the Northern Panhandle in 1794. It was the first iron furnace west of the Allegheny Mountains. In 1797, the first salt well west of the Alleghenies was drilled. It was near Charleston. In 1815, James Wilson drilled the country's first natural gas well. It, too, was near Charleston. Logging also became a big business in western Virginia. Coal had been found along the Coal River in 1742. But not until the late 1800s did coal mining become important.

The Alleghenies are part of the Appalachian Mountains.

Better transportation came to western Virginia, too. The *George Washington* was built at Wheeling in 1816. It was the country's first double-decked

The double-decked steamboat George Washington

steamboat. In 1818, the National Road reached Wheeling. It linked western Virginia with the East Coast. The first railroad train crossed western Virginia in 1853. Steamboats and trains carried people and goods to and around western Virginia. Pioneers spread across all of western Virginia during the early 1800s. By 1850, its population had reached 300,000.

The Civil War and Statehood

Western Virginia had become quite different from the rest of Virginia. Many rich farmers who owned large plantations lived in Virginia. They also owned many slaves who worked on the plantations. But most western Virginians were poor. They owned few slaves. Many opposed slavery.

John Brown's fort at Harpers Ferry National Historical Park

In 1859, western Virginia became involved in the fight against slavery. On October 16, John Brown led a raid at Harpers Ferry. He and some followers captured the United States arsenal there. That is where guns were made and stored. Brown planned to give these guns to slaves in Virginia and Maryland. He wanted to lead them to freedom.

United States soldiers retook the arsenal. They captured John Brown. Ten of his followers, including two of his sons, were killed. John Brown was tried and convicted of treason. On December 2, 1859, he was hanged at nearby Charles Town.

Abraham Lincoln was elected president in 1860. Lincoln was a northerner. Southerners feared that he would end slavery. Eleven southern states soon seceded from (left) the United States. Virginia seceded on April 17, 1861. The eleven states became the Confederate States of America.

Few western Virginians wanted to secede. In fact, many of them wanted to leave Virginia. A vote was held on October 24, 1861. By a count of 18,408 to 781, western Virginians chose to break away from Virginia. West Virginia was admitted as the thirty-fifth state on June 20, 1863. Wheeling served as the state capital.

In the meantime, the Civil War (1861-1865) had been raging for two years. West Virginia helped the Union (northern states) fight the Confederacy (southern states). The Mountain State provided about 28,000 Union troops. But another 10,000 to 12,000 West Virginians served the Confederacy. The Confederates led several raids into West Virginia. They blew up railroad tracks and bridges. One of the state's biggest battles was at Droop Mountain. Union forces defeated a southern army there on November 6, 1863.

On February 3, 1865, West Virginia abolished (ended) slavery. Nine weeks later the war ended. The defeated southern states then had to free their slaves. After the war, West Virginia had to pay Virginia about $14 million. This was for West Virginia's share of Virginia's prewar debts.

A Civil War battle being reenacted at Jackson's Mill, just north of Weston

COAL, WORLD WARS, AND DEPRESSION

In the late 1800s, West Virginia became a giant producer of coal and natural gas. Between 1910 and 1924, West Virginia led the country in mining natural gas. By 1919, it was second only to Pennsylvania at mining coal.

West Virginia had more than 9,000 coal mines by 1923.

In the early 1900s, coal miners worked long hours for little pay. Most miners lived in towns owned by the mine companies. Rents were often high for poor housing in these company towns. Coal mining was also dangerous. On December 6, 1907, 361 miners died in the Monongah Mine. This was the deadliest coal-mine explosion in United States history. In 1914, a mine disaster at Eccles claimed 188 lives.

Between 1890 and the 1920s, coal miners started banding together in unions. At times, the miners held strikes. They refused to work. Sometimes, they

A 1907 explosion at the Monongah Mine, near Fairmont (below) killed 361 miners.

fought the mine owners. In 1913, miners and company guards fought a gun battle near Charleston. Twelve miners and four guards were killed. Over the years, the miners' lives improved. Pay was raised. Hours were reduced. Mines were made safer.

In 1917, the United States entered World War I (1914-1918). West Virginia's coal was needed for the war effort. More than 45,000 West Virginians fought in the war. Newton Baker, of Martinsburg, served as President Woodrow Wilson's secretary of war (1916-1921). Huntington-born Dwight Morrow helped make the plans that won the war. Clarksburg native John Davis helped during the peace talks.

Martinsburg native Newton Baker was secretary of war during World War I. Here he is shown (blindfolded) drawing the first number in a draft lottery that chose Americans for war service.

John Davis ran for president of the United States in 1924. However, Calvin Coolidge defeated him.

Strip mining near Fairmont produced coal that helped in World War II.

The Great Depression (1929-1939) brought hard times to the United States. West Virginians suffered greatly. Farmers lost their land. Factories and mines closed. Thousands of people lost their jobs. Some mining settlements became ghost towns. The United States government started new programs. Thousands of the jobless found work. More than 60,000 West Virginians built roads, including Charleston's Kanawha Boulevard.

World War II (1939-1945) helped end the depression. The United States entered the war in 1941. West Virginia coal and steel helped the war effort. The world's largest plant for making artificial rubber was built near Charleston. Point Pleasant's shipyards made small ships. Almost 250,000 West Virginians served in the war.

RECENT CHANGES

The 1940s and 1950s were both good and bad for West Virginia. In 1947, Weirton and other settlements surrounding the Weirton Steel Company joined together. They called the new large city Weirton. Steelmaking grew. West Virginia's chemical industry boomed, too. The state had nearly fifty chemical plants by 1960. Those companies hired thousands of workers.

At the same time, the country's demand for coal dropped. Railroads switched from coal-fired engines to diesel fuel. Homes changed from coal furnaces to cleaner oil and gas heat. Nearly 70,000 West Virginia miners lost their jobs between 1948 and 1954. Thousands more have suffered the same fate since.

More coal was needed in the 1970s. But miners continued to lose their jobs. New mining machines allowed one man to do the work of four. The new machines were used in strip mining. The top layers

A 1960 picture of a West Virginia chemical plant near Charleston

25

of earth were removed to get at the coal. Strip mining is easier than digging tunnels.

Many former coal workers left West Virginia to find work. Between 1950 and 1990, West Virginia lost more than 212,000 people. It was the only state to lose population between those years.

Mining has harmed people's health and the environment. In 1972, a dam built from strip-mining waste broke. Several mining towns near Buffalo Creek flooded. The flood killed 125 people and destroyed 4,000 homes. Since then, laws have been passed to control strip mining. Mining also creates a lot of coal dust. Miners breathe it. Thousands of them have developed "black lung" disease. Some must carry oxygen tanks in case they have trouble breathing. West Virginians have the country's highest death rate from lung disease. Laws have been passed to help miners who have "black lung" disease. Waste from the mines has killed the Cheat River. Fish and plants can no longer live in it.

West Virginia faces other problems. It is one of the poorest states. The average West Virginian earns only $15,000 a year. By the mid-1990s, West Virginia had the country's highest jobless rate.

West Virginia's lawmakers and citizens are working hard for their state, however. More schools

Coal miners, Cabin Creek

West Virginia attracts many tourists who enjoy the state's beautiful mountain scenery. This hiker is on the North Bend Rail Trail, in Ritchie County.

have been built. Computers are in many of them. Teachers have received raises. New companies have been invited to West Virginia. In 1991, a bill was passed to protect the state's groundwater. West Virginia's roads have been improved. Millions of visitors drive to the state each year. Many of them are former West Virginians. They remember one of the Mountain State's other nicknames—"Almost Heaven."

West Virginians and Their Work

West Virginians and Their Work

West Virginia's population is about 1.8 million. Only sixteen states have fewer people. Thirty-three have more. Of every 100 West Virginians, 96 are white. Most of their families came from Germany, Ireland, and England. Nearly 60,000 black people live in West Virginia. About 8,000 West Virginians are of Spanish-speaking background. The Mountain State is also home to 8,000 Asian people. Almost 2,500 American Indians live in the state.

Opposite: A boy playing a mountain dulcimer during a children's folk art festival in Augusta

How West Virginians Earn Their Living

About 700,000 West Virginians have jobs. Almost 160,000 of them are service workers. They include lawyers, car repairers, and health-care workers. The Charleston Area Medical Center is a major employer. Tourism is becoming a big West Virginia service industry. Many West Virginians work in the state's hotels and motels.

Another 150,000 West Virginians sell goods. These range from cars to food. The Kroger Company is a large grocery chain. It has almost fifty

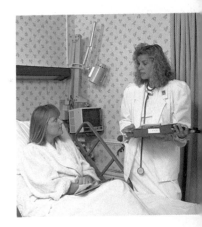

Nurses are among West Virginia's service workers.

A craftsman making art glass at the Blenko Glass Company in Milton

Unloading material at the Morgan Shirt Factory in Morgantown

stores in the state. The government employs about 130,000 West Virginians. Letter carriers and public-school teachers are in this group. So are people who work for West Virginia's government.

More than 80,000 West Virginians make goods. Chemicals are the state's top product. They include soaps, paints, and dyes. Steel, tin, aluminum, and chrome are other major products. West Virginia is also known for making fine pottery and glass. Mining machines, foods, and newsprint are other leading products.

Mining employs about 31,000 West Virginians. Only four states have more miners. West Virginia

ranks third in the country at mining coal. This is its top mining product. The state's yearly coal output is 300 billion pounds. This amounts to over 1,000 pounds of coal for each American. Natural gas, oil, and salt are other major mining products.

West Virginia has almost 25,000 farmers. The state ranks ninth in the United States at growing apples. The first Golden Delicious apples were grown in Clay County in 1912. West Virginia ranks tenth at growing peaches. Hay, corn, tobacco, cherries, pears, plums, and grapes are other important crops. Beef and dairy cattle, chickens, hogs, and sheep are major livestock products.

West Virginia is ninth among the states at growing apples.

Overleaf: Hilltop House is a 104-year-old stone inn in Harpers Ferry.

31

A Tour of the Mountain State

A Tour of the Mountain State

Visitors enjoy West Virginia's beautiful hills and mountains, valleys and rivers, caves and forests. Interesting towns and historic sites add to West Virginia's charm.

The Northern Panhandle

The Northern Panhandle is best known for its many factories. Newell is in the panhandle's northern tip. The Homer Laughlin China Company is there. This company is the world's largest dinnerware factory.

The Festival of Lights at Oglebay Resort, in Wheeling, takes place each year from November through February.

Weirton is to the south. It is the state's sixth-largest city. In 1983, Weirton Steel became the country's first employee-owned steel company. Its workers' families have come from many lands. Each summer, the city hosts the Weirton International Food and Arts Festival.

Wheeling is on the Ohio River south of Weirton. It was founded in 1769. Fort Henry was built later to protect the town. The last Revolutionary War battle was fought there in 1782. Today, in Wheeling, a plaque marks the spot where Fort Henry once stood.

Wheeling has about 35,000 people today. It is the state's third-largest city. Wheeling is another great steelmaking city. Many people take cruises on the Ohio River from Wheeling. The Good Children's Zoo is another Wheeling highlight. Native American animals including bears and snakes can be seen there.

Moundsville is south of Wheeling. It is the site of Grave Creek Mound. Ancient Indians built it over 2,000 years ago. The Palace of Gold is another Moundsville landmark. The Hare Krishna religious group built it. The ten-room palace has many interesting carvings.

A row of Victorian homes in Wheeling

The Hare Krishna palace in Moundsville

Left: Woodburn Hall, the oldest building at West Virginia University (WVU) Right: The WVU band

THE NORTH-CENTRAL REGION

Morgantown is in far northern West Virginia. It is between the Northern and Eastern Panhandles. Zackquill Morgan's town now has about 26,000 people. It is the state's fifth-largest city. Morgantown is home to West Virginia University (WVU). With about 23,000 students, WVU is the state's largest school. West Virginia trees and wildflowers are grown at WVU's Core Arboretum. Hikers may spot woodpeckers and hawks there.

Fairmont is a short drive south of Morgantown. The Marion County Museum is in Fairmont. Visitors can view rooms from five different times in West Virginia's history. The Miner's Memorial is outside Fairmont. It is near the site of the 1907 Monongah Mine explosion. The memorial honors those who have died in mining accidents.

West Virginia had more than 20,000 mining deaths between 1883 and 1993.

Terra Alta is west of Fairmont. The Americana Museum is in this town. Visitors can see a blacksmith shop, country store, and doctor's office there. Clarksburg is south of Fairmont. This city was Civil War general Stonewall Jackson's birthplace. Today, his statue stands in front of the courthouse. Clarksburg's Waldomore Madison Museum has displays on UFOs (flying saucers). West of Clarksburg is Salem, home to Fort New Salem. Twenty West Virginia log cabins were rebuilt there.

Terra Alta means "high ground."

THE EASTERN PANHANDLE

Much of West Virginia's early history started in the Eastern Panhandle. George Washington enjoyed the warm waters at Berkeley Springs in 1747. In 1756, the country's first public mineral springs resort opened there. Berkeley Springs is still a popular health resort.

Waldomore Madison Museum, in Clarksburg

Harpers Ferry

A view of Harpers Ferry and the Shenandoah River

Martinsburg is to the southeast. It is the Eastern Panhandle's largest city. About 14,000 people live there. Revolutionary War general Adam Stephen founded this city in 1778. The General Adam Stephen House dates from 1789. Many visitors stay in Martinsburg's old inns. One of them is Boydville. It is a mansion nearly 200 years old.

Nearby, to the east, is Shepherdstown. Called Mecklenburg until 1798, it was West Virginia's first town. The Historic Shepherdstown Museum tells visitors about the town's early years. The town has three other claims to fame. In 1787, the world's first steamboat was launched there on the Potomac.

In 1790, West Virginia's first newspaper was published at Mecklenburg. Also in 1790, George Washington suggested the town for the United States capital. Washington, D.C., was chosen instead.

South of Shepherdstown is Harpers Ferry. Harpers Ferry was named for Robert Harper. In the 1700s, he ran a ferryboat. It carried people across the Potomac and Shenandoah rivers. Today, many Harpers Ferry buildings have been restored. They look as they did when John Brown made his raid in 1859. The buildings are part of Harpers Ferry National Historical Park. Visitors can learn about John Brown. They can also see what an 1850s town was like.

Nearby is Charles Town. John Brown was tried and hanged there. Three stones mark the spot where he died. Charles Town was founded in 1786 by Charles Washington. He was George Washington's youngest brother. Charles's home is called Happy Retreat. Harewood House was built for Samuel Washington. He was another Washington brother. Bushrod Washington was George Washington's nephew. He built a beautiful house called Claymont Court. All the Washington homes can be seen today. Some are open to the

James and Dolley Madison were married at Harewood House (above) in 1794. Madison was the fourth president of the United States (1809-1817).

The National Radio Astronomy Observatory, in Green Bank

An event at the West Virginia State Fair

public. Descendants of George Washington still live in Charles Town to this day.

Romney is in the western part of the Eastern Panhandle. Ice Mountain is not far from Romney. Ice fills cracks in this mountain during the winter. Some ice remains even on the hottest summer days. Far to the southwest in the panhandle is Seneca Rocks. This sandstone rock formation rises 960 feet. It is a hard test for rock climbers. Spruce Knob rises near Seneca Rocks. This is West Virginia's highest peak. Visitors can drive to its top.

SOUTHEASTERN WEST VIRGINIA

South of Spruce Knob is Green Bank. The National Radio Astronomy Observatory is there. Its radio telescopes gather radio waves from faraway stars. From them, scientists learn more about the universe. The Cass Scenic Railroad is nearby. Long ago, this was a logging railroad. Today, it carries tourists. The railroad goes to the top of Bald Knob. That is the state's second-highest peak.

White Sulphur Springs is farther south. Its mineral springs have made it a famous resort town. Nearby Lewisburg hosts the State Fair each August. The fair lasts nine days. Farm exhibits, music, and

40

food are featured. Famous West Virginians take part in a cow-milking contest.

The Mountain State has many caves. Lost World Caverns is near Lewisburg. Some of its formations look like waterfalls, owls, and alligators. Organ Cave is also near Lewisburg. One of its formations looks like organ pipes. When struck, it makes musical tones.

The Big Bend Tunnels are to the west. They are railroad tunnels that were built in the 1870s. These tunnels were blasted through mountains. It was there that the story of John Henry started. John Henry was a black railroad worker. He hammered holes in mountainsides. Explosives were placed in the holes to blast away the mountain. Henry could work faster than a steel drill. Stories and songs were written about his contest with the drill. Today, the John Henry Statue stands near the tunnels.

West of the tunnels is Beckley. The Exhibition Coal Mine is there. Former coal miners take visitors through the mine's underground tunnels. The Coal Museum is next to the mine. There, visitors can learn about the history of coal mining. Each August, Beckley hosts the Appalachian Arts & Crafts Festival. Visitors can watch quilters, wood-carvers, potters, and glassmakers at work.

The John Henry Statue near Big Bend Tunnels

The Exhibition Coal Mine in Beckley

41

A rock climber at the New River Gorge National Recreation Area

CENTRAL WEST VIRGINIA

The New River Gorge Bridge stands outside Fayetteville. This is the world's longest steel-arch bridge. It is 1,700 feet long. The bridge towers 876 feet above the New River. On Bridge Day each October, the bridge is closed to cars. People can walk on the bridge and enjoy the view below. There, the New River rushes through a canyon. That part of the river is called New River Gorge National River. People white-water raft and canoe on the river. Hawks Nest State Park is also near Fayetteville. It offers great views of the river.

To the north is Summersville. South of town is Summersville Dam. The dam is nearly half a mile long. It is 390 feet high. The dam created Summersville Lake. Many people enjoy boating, fishing, and swimming there. Others hike around the lake or picnic by its shores.

Charleston is west of Summersville Lake. With more than 57,000 people, Charleston is West Virginia's largest city. It is also West Virginia's capital. The state capitol's golden dome is 293 feet high. The Capitol in Washington, D.C., is not quite that high. The West Virginia State Museum is near the capitol. There, visitors can see a settler's cabin and an old general store. Charleston's Sunrise Museum is housed in two buildings. One exhibits American artworks. The other has science exhibits and a planetarium. Each May, Charleston hosts the Vandalia Gathering. Folk songs are played on fiddles, banjos, and mountain dulcimers.

SOME WESTERN HIGHLIGHTS

Milton is west of Charleston. This town has one of West Virginia's many covered bridges. The Mud River Bridge dates from 1876. Milton's Blenko

A musician at the Vandalia Gathering

The capitol, in Charleston

Glass Company is well-known. Stained-glass windows made there are in churches around the world. The Country Music Award is made there. Visitors to the plant can watch glassblowers at work.

To the west, on the Ohio River, is Huntington. This city started as a railroad town in 1871. Today, Huntington has about 55,000 people. That makes it the state's second-largest city. The Huntington Museum of Art is the state's biggest art museum. European and American paintings hang there. Also on display are glass objects made in the Ohio River Valley. Train lovers enjoy Heritage Village. This is a restored 1880s train station. Children can climb on a train car there.

Heritage Village, a restored 1880s train station, in Huntington

Farther north along the Ohio River lies Point Pleasant. Point Pleasant Battle Monument rises above the state park there. Chief Cornstalk is buried there. The West Virginia State Farm Museum is near Point Pleasant. This museum has thirty-five pioneer buildings. They include a log church, a schoolhouse, and a country store.

Parkersburg lies still farther north on the Ohio River. Settled in 1785, it is the state's fourth-largest city. Parkersburg has almost 34,000 people. William Stevenson's home is in Parkersburg's historic district. Stevenson was the state's third governor.

From Parkersburg, stern-wheelers take passengers to Blennerhassett Island. It is in the Ohio River. This is a good place to end a tour of West Virginia. In 1800, Harman Blennerhassett completed a mansion on the island. In 1806, he was part of a plot against the United States government. Blennerhassett was arrested and his home was seized. In 1811, a fire destroyed the house. Since then, the mansion has been rebuilt. After touring the house, visitors can take a horse-drawn wagon ride on the island.

Blennerhassett Mansion

A Gallery of Famous West Virginians

A Gallery of Famous West Virginians

There have been many famous West Virginians. They include lawmakers, athletes, and authors of children's books.

Martin Delany (1812-1885) was born in Charles Town. He became one of the country's first black surgeons. Dr. Delany also helped slaves escape northward to freedom. In 1847, he helped found *The North Star.* This was one of the country's first newspapers especially for black people. During the Civil War, Delany recruited black troops for the Union. He became the country's first black army major.

Another great black leader was **Booker T. Washington** (1856-1915). He was born in Virginia. Washington was freed from slavery at age nine. He then moved with his mother to Malden, West Virginia. There, Washington worked in a salt furnace and then a coal mine. Finally, he became a teacher. In 1881, he founded a school for black students in Alabama. It is called Tuskegee University.

Thomas "Stonewall" Jackson (1824-1863) was born in Clarksburg. He, too, was a teacher. Later, he became a Confederate Civil War general.

Delany was the grandson of an African prince.

Opposite: Booker T. Washington

Jackson fought bravely against great odds in the Battle of Bull Run (1861). Another general said that Jackson held his ground "like a stone wall." He was called Stonewall Jackson after that.

Belle Boyd (1843-1900) was born in Martinsburg. When she was seventeen, Boyd became a Confederate spy. She carried messages to Confederate camps. She also nursed wounded soldiers. Once, she saved Stonewall Jackson from capture. Boyd was later captured herself. She married the Union officer who guarded her.

Walter Reuther (1907-1970) was born in Wheeling. When he was fifteen, Reuther went to work for a steel company. He helped start the United Automobile Workers (UAW) in 1935. From 1946 to 1970, he led this Michigan-based union. Reuther helped auto workers win higher pay and better working conditions.

Cyrus Vance was born in Clarksburg in 1917. He became a statesman. Vance was U.S. secretary of state (1977-1980) for President Jimmy Carter. Over the years, he has worked to settle conflicts around the world. In 1993-94, Vance tried to work out a peace plan for Bosnia.

Cyrus Vance

Robert Byrd

Robert C. Byrd was born in North Carolina in 1918. He grew up on a West Virginia farm. Byrd became a popular West Virginia lawmaker. He has been a U.S. senator since 1959. Byrd twice has served as Senate majority leader (1977-1981 and 1987-1989). He is also known for his fiddle playing.

George Crumb was born in Charleston in 1929. He became a composer. Crumb has used West Virginia folk songs in his works. In some of his pieces, the musicians whistle. They also play on handsaws and pot lids. Crumb won the 1968 Pulitzer Prize in music for *Echoes of Time and the River*.

Ada Beatrice Queen Victoria Louise Virginia Smith (1894-1984) was born in Alderson. She had

African and Irish backgrounds. Smith was called "Bricktop" because of her red hair. Bricktop became a famous singer in the United States and Europe. She also raised money for children orphaned by World War II.

Actor **Don Knotts** was born in Morgantown in 1924. He won five Emmy Awards as Deputy Barney Fife on "The Andy Griffith Show." Knotts also made many movies. One of them was *The Apple Dumpling Gang.*

Chuck Yeager was born at Myra in 1923. He was a World War II fighter pilot. Later, he became a

Chuck Yeager

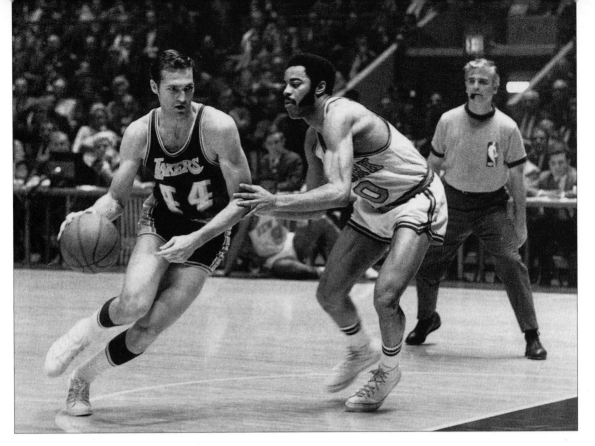

test pilot. In 1947, Yeager set a speed record. He became the first pilot to fly faster than the speed of sound. Today, Charleston's airport is named for him.

Jerry West (on the left) played with the Los Angeles Lakers

Jerry West was born in Chelyan in 1938. West was an All-American basketball player at West Virginia University. Then he played with the Los Angeles Lakers. He was the first player to score over 4,000 playoff points.

The Mountain State has produced some baseball stars, too. **Jesse Burkett** (1870-1953) was born in Wheeling. He hit over .400 in three seasons. Only two other big leaguers have done that. Burkett entered the Baseball Hall of Fame in 1946. **George Brett** was born in Glen Dale in 1953. Brett had 3,154 major league hits. He is eleventh for all-time hits. **John Kruk** was born in Charleston in 1961. He grew up in Keyser. His dad was his Little League coach. Kruk is a great hitter. He led the Philadelphia Phillies to the 1993 National League pennant.

Mary Lou Retton was born in Fairmont in 1968. She became a champion gymnast. At the 1984 Summer Olympics, Retton won five medals in gymnastics.

Many authors have come from West Virginia. **Pearl S. Buck** (1892-1973) was born in Hillsboro. She grew up in China. Her parents were missionaries there. By age ten, Buck was selling stories to a newspaper. She became a great writer. Her best-known novel is *The Good Earth*. It is about a Chinese family. In 1938, Buck won the Nobel Prize in literature. No American woman had won this award before.

Jean Lee Latham was born in Buckhannon in 1902. Latham made up stories before she could read. When she grew up, Latham wrote books for children. Her *Carry On, Mr. Bowditch* won the 1956 Newbery Medal. **Betsy Byars,** another children's author, was born in North Carolina in 1928. Byars

George Brett

Pearl Buck

later moved to West Virginia. Several of her books are set there. Byars won the 1971 Newbery Medal for *The Summer of the Swans.*

Birthplace of Pearl S. Buck, Cyrus Vance, Chuck Yeager, Martin Delany, and Bricktop . . .

Home, too, of Booker T. Washington, Robert C. Byrd, and Betsy Byars . . .

The site of John Brown's raid and John Henry's contest with a machine . . .

A state famous for mining coal, growing apples, and making glass . . .

This is the Mountain State—West Virginia!

Did You Know?

West Virginia has the country's biggest eastern hemlock tree. The giant at Aurora is 123 feet tall. Its trunk is 19 feet around.

Barbara Jo Rubin achieved two horse-racing firsts in 1969. On February 22 at Charles Town, the nineteen-year-old became the first woman jockey to win a race on a regular U.S. track. On March 8 at Chester, she became the first woman jockey in the country to ride two winners in one day.

Buckhannon hosts the West Virginia Strawberry Festival each May. Children judge the Sweetest Strawberry Contest. There are parades, strawberry ice cream, and the crowning of a Strawberry Queen and King.

The town of Hundred was named in honor of resident Henry Church. He was called "Old Hundred." Church died in 1860 at the age of 109. His wife lived to be 106.

To build Charleston's airport, the tops of mountains were chopped off. Valleys were then filled with dirt to make runways.

Coal House in White Sulphur Springs is thought to be the world's only home made completely of coal.

Many of West Virginia's towns have odd names. In fact, the state has a town named Odd. Bozoo, Duck, Echo, Friendly, Junior, Man, Left Hand, Thursday, Pickle Street, Windy, Quick, Volcano, Pinch, Looneyville, and Pie are other West Virginia towns.

In 1988, West Virginia lawmakers enacted a "No Pass, No Drive" law. Students under eighteen who drop out of school lose their driver's license. In the law's first year, the number of dropouts fell by about 1,500.

Mary Harris Jones was a famous labor leader. She joined the miner's struggle in West Virginia. The miners called her "Mother Jones." This brave woman led marches and faced machine guns. When she was jailed in 1913 for leading a West Virginia coal strike, Mother Jones was eighty-three. Ten years later, she was still working on behalf of West Virginia coal miners.

The state also has towns named Cinderella and Pumpkintown.

West Virginia is west of most of Virginia. But Virginia's western tip actually extends west of West Virginia.

The town of Grafton held the first Mother's Day in 1908. Anna Jarvis of Grafton felt there should be a holiday honoring mothers. The custom spread. In 1915, Mother's Day became a national holiday.

West Virginia Information

State flag

Rhododendron

Cardinal

Area: 24,231 square miles (forty-first among the states in size)

Greatest Distance North to South: 237 miles

Greatest Distance East to West: 265 miles

Borders: Pennsylvania and Maryland to the north and east; Virginia to the south and southeast; Kentucky to the southwest; Ohio to the northwest

Highest Point: Spruce Knob, 4,863 feet above sea level

Lowest Point: 240 feet above sea level, along the Potomac River in Jefferson County

Hottest Recorded Temperature: 112° F. (at Moorefield, on August 4, 1930, and at Martinsburg, on July 10, 1936)

Coldest Recorded Temperature: -37° F. (at Lewisburg, on December 30, 1917)

Statehood: The thirty-fifth state, on June 20, 1863

Origin of Name: West Virginia was formed from fifty western counties in Virginia, which had been named for England's Queen Elizabeth I, the "Virgin Queen"

Capital: Charleston (the permanent capital since 1885)

Previous Capitals: Wheeling (1863-1870 and 1875-1885) and Charleston (1870-1875)

Counties: 55

United States Representatives: 3 (as of 1992)

State Senators: 34

State Delegates: 100

State Songs: "The West Virginia Hills," by Ellen King (words) and H. E. Engle (music); "This Is My West Virginia," by Iris Bell; "West Virginia, My Home Sweet Home," by Julian G. Hearne, Jr.

State Motto: *Montani Semper Liberi* (Latin, meaning "Mountaineers Are Always Free")

Nicknames: "Mountain State," " Almost Heaven," "Panhandle State"

State Seal: Adopted in 1863

State Flag: Adopted in 1929

State Colors: Blue and gold

State Flower: Rhododendron

State Tree: Sugar maple

State Bird: Cardinal

State Animal: Black bear

State Fish: Brook trout

State Fruit: Apple

Black bear

State Day: June 20, the anniversary of statehood (West Virginia Day)

Some Rivers: Ohio, Potomac, Kanawha, Little Kanawha, New, Greenbrier, Cheat, Tygart Valley, Monongahela, Big Sandy, Guyandotte, Tug Fork, Shenandoah

Some Lakes: Sutton, Summersville, Bluestone, Tygart

Mountains: Allegheny

Wildlife: Black bears, white-tailed deer, foxes, opossums, skunks, raccoons, groundhogs, cardinals, eagles, owls, hawks, crows, cat-birds, woodpeckers, many other kinds of birds, garter snakes and other snakes, brook trout, bass, catfish, walleyed pike, many other kinds of fish, turtles, lizards

Manufactured Products: Detergents, paints, steel, tin, glassware, pottery, rubber, lumber and wood products, mining machinery, baked goods

Farm Products: Apples, peaches, hay, corn, tobacco, cherries, pears, grapes, beef cattle, dairy cows, chickens, hogs, sheep

Mining Products: Coal, natural gas, oil, salt, crushed stone, sand and gravel

Population: 1,793,477, thirty-fourth among the states (1990 U.S. Census Bureau figures)

Sugar maple

Apples

Major Cities (1990 Census):

City	Population	City	Population
Charleston	57,287	Weirton	22,124
Huntington	54,844	Fairmont	20,210
Wheeling	34,882	Beckley	18,296
Parkersburg	33,862	Clarksburg	18,059
Morgantown	25,879	Martinsburg	14,073

West Virginia History

The B & O Railroad tracks had to cut through many western Virginia mountains.

14,000 B.C.—The first people reach the West Virginia area

1607—Virginia, which included present-day West Virginia, is settled as the first of England's thirteen American colonies

1669-70—John Lederer explores near present-day Harpers Ferry for Virginia's English governor

1671—Thomas Batts and Robert Fallam lead an expedition along the New River

1727—German people from Pennsylvania begin Mecklenburg, now called Shepherdstown

1731—Morgan ap Morgan begins the town of Bunker Hill

1742—Coal is found along West Virginia's Coal River

1767—Zackquill Morgan, son of Morgan ap Morgan, begins Morgantown

1774—Settlers defeat the Shawnee at the Battle of Point Pleasant, ending Lord Dunmore's War

1775-83—About 1,300 western Virginians help the United States win the Revolutionary War against England

1794—Charleston is founded

1815—The country's first natural gas well is drilled near Charleston

1816—The *George Washington,* the country's first double-decked steamboat, is built at Wheeling

1853—West Virginia's first railroad train arrives in Wheeling

1859—On October 16, John Brown raids the U.S. arsenal at Harpers Ferry

1861-65—About 28,000 West Virginians help the Union win the Civil War

1863—West Virginia becomes the thirty-fifth state on June 20

1865—West Virginia ends slavery on February 3

1871—Huntington is begun

1872—West Virginia adopts a state constitution that is still in effect

1885—Charleston becomes the permanent capital

1907—An explosion at the Monongah Mine kills 361

1908—Anna Jarvis of Grafton arranges the first Mother's Day celebration

1917-18—West Virginia sends 45,000 soldiers to help the United States win World War I

1928—Minnie Buckingham Harper is appointed to the West Virginia House of Delegates, becoming the first black woman member of a U.S. legislative body

1929-39—The Great Depression hurts coal mining, farming, and manufacturing in West Virginia

1941-45—About 250,000 West Virginians serve in the armed forces to help the United States win World War II

1954—The West Virginia Turnpike is completed

1959—The National Radio Astronomy Observatory opens at Green Bank

1969—The U.S. Congress passes a law designed to protect the health and safety of U.S. coal miners

1972—The collapse of a dam made from strip-mining waste causes a flood that kills 125 people along Buffalo Creek

1985—A lottery is created to raise money for West Virginia

1989—Gaston Caperton becomes governor and makes many changes that help the state

1990—West Virginia's population is 1,793,477

1991—West Virginia passes a law to protect the state's groundwater

1992—Gaston Caperton is reelected governor

1993—Two thousand coal workers join the United Mine Workers Strike

1995—The U.S. Supreme Court upholds the state's ban on minority scholarships in public universities

Anna Jarvis

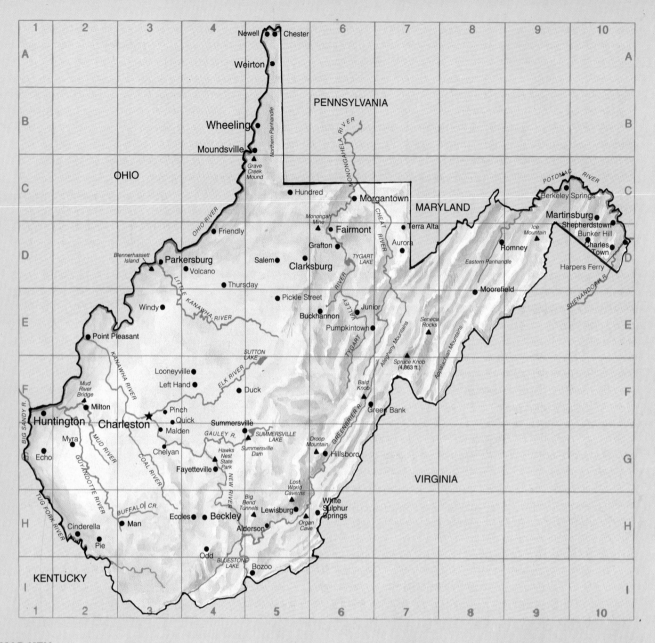

GLOSSARY

ancient: Related to a time long ago

arboretum: An outdoor setting where trees and other plants are grown so they can be studied

arsenal: A place where weapons are made and stored

artificial: Not occurring naturally; made by people

billion: A thousand million (1,000,000,000)

capital: The city that is the seat of government

capitol: The building in which the government meets

colony: A settlement that is outside a parent country and ruled by that country

depression: A period of hard times

environment: The surroundings of a person or a place

explorer: A person who visits and studies unknown lands

flash flood: A flood that occurs quickly and with little or no warning after a heavy rain

million: A thousand thousand (1,000,000)

mountain dulcimer: A sweet-sounding stringed instrument created long ago by people in the Appalachian Mountains

panhandle: A piece of land shaped like the handle of a pan

permanent: Lasting

pioneer: A person who is among the first to move into a region

planetarium: A machine that shows images of the stars and planets on the ceiling of a special building

plantation: A large farm

secede: To withdraw from, or leave

strip mining: Coal mining in which the top levels of earth are torn away to reach the coal

tourism: The business of providing services such as food and lodging for travelers

UFO: An Unidentified Flying Object, often called a flying saucer

union: A group that helps working people

A Foggy valley in Braxton County, early in the morning

PICTURE ACKNOWLEDGMENTS

62

INDEX

Page numbers in boldface type indicate illustrations.

ABOUT THE AUTHORS

Dennis and Judith Fradin have coauthored several books in the From Sea to Shining Sea series. The Fradins both graduated from Northwestern University in 1967. Dennis has been a professional writer for twenty years, and has published 150 books. His works for Childrens Press include the Young People's Stories of Our States series, the Disaster! series, and the Thirteen Colonies series. Judith earned her M.A. in literature from Northwestern University and taught high-school and college English for many years. The Fradins, who are the parents of Anthony, Diana, and Michael, live in Evanston, Illinois.